Your Aptitudes

You Do Best What You Are Best Fitted to Do

George Francis Barth

Your Aptitudes

You Do Best What You Are Best Fitted To Do

Consultant
Carl M. Tausig, Ed.D.,
Research Specialist
Enrichment of Teacher and Counselor
Competencies in Career Education
Center for Educational Studies
Eastern Illinois University
Charleston, Illinois

2492

Lothrop, Lee & Shepard Co.
New York

Printed in the United States of America.

1   2   3   4   5   78   77   76   75   74

Library of Congress Cataloging in Publication Data

Barth, George Francis.
    Your aptitudes; you do best what you are best suited to do.

    SUMMARY: Leads the reader to consider his own abilities through a discussion of nineteen aptitudes important in today's job market.
    1. Occupational aptitude tests—Juvenile literature.   2. Vocational in-terests—Juvenile literature.   [1. Occupational aptitude tests.   2. Voca-tional guidance]   I. Title.

HF5381.2.B35   371.2′62   74-10875

ISBN 0-688-41651-9

Contents

Introduction

Have you thought about your future? Do you know what kind of work you would like to do? And, more important, do you know if it is the kind you are best fitted to do? If you do know, you probably will be successful and happy doing it.

Otherwise you may find yourself drifting into one kind of work or another, purely by chance. If it happens to suit you, all may go well. If not, you are less likely to enjoy success and happiness. Now is the time to learn all you can about yourself. It is possible that a job that holds appeal for you is really not the right one for you at all.

A boy named Bruce was thirteen and ready to enter high school. He was a good ballplayer and enjoyed listening to the radio sports announcers. He told his father he wanted to become a sports announcer.

His father was glad his son was thinking about his future. But he suggested that Bruce should learn more about himself before he made up his mind about his future career. "Do you know if you have the aptitudes to be a good sports announcer?" his father asked.

Bruce was puzzled. He hadn't thought about aptitudes. In fact, he didn't know what they were. He quickly learned that everyone is born with certain talents and capabilities, the natural tendencies that enable us to do some things better than others.

Bruce's school had no vocational guidance counselor, so his father brought him to an aptitude-testing laboratory in New York City. To his surprise Bruce learned that his combination of aptitudes pointed to a career in engineering. He had few of the aptitudes called for in a sports-announcing job.

At first Bruce was disappointed. But, as he learned more about aptitudes, he accepted the advice to study engineering. Today he is a successful chemical engineer, happy with his work and with himself.

What would have happened if Bruce refused that advice and tried to become a sports announcer? Could he have made it? Possibly, but the chances were great that he would have failed in this kind of work.

Before you make a decision about your career, try to learn as much as you can about yourself and your aptitudes. Remember, aptitudes, like muscles, have to be developed. One person with an aptitude for drawing may work at it and become an artist. Another, with just as much or even more ability, may dabble at drawing for a while, then lose interest.

An aptitude that is not encouraged can wither away. With aptitudes, it is not always a case of either having them or not. The person we call an "underachiever" may be one who has aptitudes but, for some reason, lacks the drive to develop and use them. For instance, a person with little natural athletic ability may enjoy playing tennis. By practice and persistence, this person may play a better game than someone with more athletic ability who gets little practice.

To return to our example, Bruce learned that his strongest aptitudes would lead him toward engineering. However, his interest in sports wasn't ignored. He developed this interest as a hobby. He became an expert bowler and a great sports fan. In this way he made use of all his aptitudes—and felt fulfilled.

It's a good idea, then, to learn what your aptitudes are, and to get to know yourself better. You may discover talents that you never knew you had. And you will be better able to make the right decision about the kind of work to choose.

Knowing that you have the right combination of aptitudes for a particular career will give you self-confidence. This can strengthen the urge to attain your goal that Psychologist William James described by saying that if you wish for something hard enough, and wish for it exclusively, you will eventually get it!

There are many different tests for aptitudes, which are not always given the same names. This book will describe the nineteen aptitudes for which Bruce was tested. They are considered important in today's job market. As you read about them, you will probably see why you are better at doing certain jobs while your friend may be better at doing different ones.

No book can take the place of actual tests. Nevertheless,

it is important to know what aptitudes are. Then you will understand why you do best what you are best fitted to do, and you will see the truth of the old saying: "You can't fit a square peg into a round hole."

No one has all the aptitudes described and no one is expected to be good at doing everything. Everyone has a *combination* of some of the aptitudes. Perhaps you will discover that you have more abilities than you thought. If you do, you will probably develop new interests and hobbies and new skills. These could add greatly to your self-confidence.

1 · What Is Your Personality Pattern?

Personality is a very complex subject. No two persons, any more than two fingerprints, are exactly alike. If you were tested by a school counselor, he or she would probably want to learn your *interest in ideas,* your *interest in artistic things, how independent you are, whether you act impulsively, if you are anxious very often,* and so on. None of these personality traits can be tested in a book. But one basic trait must be considered when you are deciding on a career. This is whether you are mainly *introverted* or mainly *extroverted.* This is sometimes called "subjective" and "objective."

After many years of testing, it has been found that about three-quarters of us belong to the extroverted type. The remaining one-quarter belongs to the introverted type. No one is completely one or the other. And often an extroverted person will have a hobby or interest that is introverted in nature. However, everyone tends to be more one way than the other. Neither type should be considered better than the other. There are successful and happy people of both kinds. Society needs both. What is important is to try to learn whether you are more one than the other.

Generally, the extroverted person enjoys working with others more than working alone. A good example is the salesperson, especially one who is successful in cold canvassing. This person must be tough enough to be able to take rebuffs. He or she cannot be too sensitive or shy or self-conscious.

This doesn't mean that *only* extroverts can succeed in selling jobs. It depends on the kind of selling and on the selling "climate." When a buyer calls the salesperson in, for example, the introverted person who knows the product well may be very successful. Here the selling "climate" is completely different. Whether a sale is made or not, no doors will be slammed in the person's face, as is often the case in cold canvassing.

Extroverted persons are usually outgoing. Business executives who manage large groups of people are often extroverts. They enjoy directing people as a rule. Politicians, tour guides, masters of ceremonies, hosts and hostesses, to mention just a few, do best if they are extroverted. They are all doing work that keeps them in constant touch with others.

Introverted persons tend to live more within themselves. Painters, poets, composers, and other people who spend most of their time alone in their work, thinking, dreaming, creating, are behaving subjectively. So, usually, are designers and research scientists. Those who are skilled in giving advice, as in medicine, psychology, or law, are generally introverted. Again, this is *not* to say that extroverts couldn't

An introverted person may be happy doing work that requires being alone.

do their kind of work. They can and do, but extroverted persons in such fields tend to become administrators or directors. Their outgoing personalities often propel them out of more solitary situations into spots where they are more in contact with others. This is especially true of those with a large vocabulary—but more on vocabulary later.

There is no reason why introverted and extroverted persons cannot do the same work. The point to consider is which job is most suitable in terms of aptitudes and most satisfying in terms of personality patterns.

Any career that you consider for yourself will demand certain requirements. These will include your combination of aptitudes and acquired skills. Special training and education may also be needed. However, the first consideration is whether the job is better suited to the introverted or the extroverted person. Bruce, who wanted to become a sportscaster, probably would have been unsuccessful in that job. Why? Because by nature he was introverted and a sportscaster who is extroverted is better suited for such a career.

Bruce became a successful chemical engineer because he had the right combination of aptitudes, as well as the right personality pattern for his engineering job. It is interesting to note that part of his job now calls for selling. His customers seek his advice in a professional, scientific situation. He is successful because the selling "climate" suits his personality.

If the career you have in mind will keep you mostly to yourself, or in a one-to-one relationship as a doctor, counselor, or whatever, then it would be best if you were mostly introvert. However, if the job entails contact with others, then you would do well if you are mostly extrovert. To help you decide whether you are mostly introverted or mostly extroverted, see if you seem to fit either of the following descriptions:

The introverted person is often quiet, sensitive, shy and self-conscious. He or she may avoid being the center of attention. Introverted persons are often individualists. They tend to feel deeply. If, through writing, painting, music or acting, they can project these feelings, they can move others to feel, also.

Introverted persons often become professionals—doctors, counselors, lawyers, psychologists, artists and writers. They deal usually with one person at a time, or they work alone. Still others seek jobs in offices, such as typing, doing clerical work, keeping records, bookkeeping, and so on. But this doesn't mean that only introverted persons like office jobs.

Introverted people often lean toward designing, laboratory testing, scientific research, and similar jobs in which they can achieve satisfaction working alone. In factories they can be content doing piecework, or bench-assembly work, by themselves.

Highly extroverted persons are easy mixers. They like, and actually need, to be with others. Working alone bores them. They are more likely to conform and be like their peers as much as possible. The jobs they enjoy doing most are those where they are meeting others, or are in frequent contact with others. Selling jobs are typical.

Whether you are introverted or extroverted, the important point to consider is whether the job calls for your combination of aptitudes. The next thing to consider is the kind of job that would give you the most satisfaction and happiness in the doing.

If the extrovert has the same aptitudes as the introvert, there is nothing to prevent him or her from doing the same kind of work. In such a case, and depending on their vocabulary and other aptitudes, these persons may become dissatisfied with the isolation of working alone. Accordingly, they may strive to become administrators, teachers, or directors, in whatever field they enter.

What is your personality pattern? Whatever you think you are, don't waste time wishing that you were different. One kind of personality is no better or worse than another. What is important is to know yourself. Toward that end, be guided by these descriptions, for they will help you to be yourself!

2 · Do You Like Paper Work?

Did you keep a neat notebook in school? Did you prepare your homework papers in a neat and orderly way? Do you find it easy to keep records, notes, files, and to compile figures? Are the papers in your desk arranged so that you can get at anything you need easily? If all this comes to you naturally, the chances are that you may rate high in *accounting aptitude*—the ability to handle all kinds of figures and paper work.

Both introverted and extroverted persons may need this aptitude in their work. Nurses, for example, are usually best if they are extroverted. They need paper work skill to keep accurate records of a patient's temperature, pulse rate, blood pressure, medications, and the like. Introverted persons with this aptitude enjoy working alone on figures, statistics, records, paper work. But there is no hard-and-fast rule. Both personality types can and do rate high in this aptitude.

A great many jobs make use of this aptitude. The obvious ones include accounting, bookkeeping, clerical work, stenography, secretarial work, also laboratory work where

accurate records of tests are kept. Any office work that involves records and papers of all sorts calls for accounting aptitude. Incidentally, this aptitude bears no relationship to intelligence. Many talented, even brilliant, people are low in this aptitude while others can score very high. Musicians, for example, must be high in this skill. It enables them to read music easily.

Can you judge yourself in this aptitude? Think about your school experience. Remember the paper work you had to handle, both in class and at home. Were you at ease when using figures? Were you neat and did you do this kind of work well? Did you find the actual writing of figures, as well as the arranging of papers, easy, perhaps interesting?

How do you stand now? Do you have a checkbook? If so, do you keep it properly recorded and balanced, so that you know exactly the amount of money on deposit at all times? Actually, few persons are able to keep accurate checkbook records.

Are you in the habit of making notes, not only for yourself, but for others? Do you like clerical work in an office, keeping records and compiling figures? Any or all of these are fair indicators of this aptitude. If you judge yourself fairly, you may be able to decide whether you would rate high or low in accounting aptitude.

People with an aptitude for accounting handle records and other paper work with ease. *Oscar Meyer & Co.*

3 · Do You Have Lots of Ideas?

Would you say you have a good imagination? Do all sorts of ideas come easily to you? When you are describing something that happened, do you find yourself stretching things a little to make the story more interesting or exciting? If you are in a debate, or just plain arguing, are you able to come up with reason after reason why you are right and the other person is wrong? Suppose you were given part of a story and were asked to finish it. If you did this very well, you could possibly rate high in *creative imagination*—the ability to develop ideas.

This is an aptitude that is called for in many kinds of work. Salespeople, for instance, have to be quick with ideas, suggestions, explanations, that fit the needs of many different kinds of people. Writers, of course, must score high. This applies to writers of advertising, promotion, public relations, as well as to writers of scenarios, novels, and short stories.

Trial lawyers need this aptitude to plead successfully before the bar. Politicians, preachers, psychological counselors, cartoonists need it, too. Even physical therapists should have good imaginations, for they must often invent ways of adapting their training methods to help handicapped people. Teachers need this aptitude to create interesting learning situations and to stimulate the imaginations of their students.

Imagination is an asset in a salesperson demonstrating a product.
Allis-Chalmers Corp.

Some jobs do not require this aptitude. Too much imagination can make it difficult to concentrate on the work in hand. Accountants and bookkeepers, generally, do not need it when they are concentrating on their facts and figures. However, persons in this field who do have creative imaginations, perhaps combined with an extrovert personality, may be spurred toward becoming managers, administrators, or executives. Accountants of this kind sometimes rise to the top of their companies. With a flow of ideas and a knowledge of facts and figures, they often make fine executives.

There are some jobs where this aptitude is not helpful. Since a creative imagination tends to make the mind wander, it makes it difficult, sometimes, to concentrate on the work at hand. This applies to dentists or surgeons whose work demands that they concentrate wholly on what they are doing. It also applies to the factory bench-assembly worker who is concentrating on many small parts. Of course, when such persons try to invent something, or develop a better technique, a creative imagination is very useful.

The introverted person with this talent could use it in many different kinds of jobs; for example, in writing, research work, designing, and inventing. For those who take up engineering this aptitude could make them more creative. They would be better able to develop or invent new ideas and applications within their field.

An extroverted person with this aptitude might use it in a variety of jobs—teaching, selling, job training, or being a disc jockey. There are hundreds of jobs for the extrovert blessed with a constant flow of ideas.

How do you think you rate? If you answered "yes" to the questions at the beginning of this chapter, you could possibly rate high. If not, perhaps you should ask your relatives or friends to help you decide.

4 · Can You Think in Three Dimensions?

Are you mechanically inclined? Did you ever model in clay, fold paper into box-like shapes, or use other kinds of material to make objects that were solid or three-dimensional? Can you take apart a toy or a toaster, or something else that needs fixing, and put it together again without much trouble? If your answer is "yes," then the chances are that you might score high in *concrete thinking*—the ability to think about or imagine real objects that are solid or three-dimensional.

The architect is a good example of a person who must be able to visualize solid objects or structures. Civil engineers, who build bridges and highways, work with solids or three-dimensional objects. So do mechanical engineers who design and build machines. The diemaker, who makes patterns and molds, must be able to visualize the finished product his die will produce. The sculptor, too, must be able to "see" the finished statue in his or her imagination. Surgeons

A high score in concrete thinking is a plus for a construction worker.

must have a clear picture in mind of the structure of that part of the body on which they are operating. The same is true of the builder, the mechanic, the dressmaker, the fashion designer—anyone whose job deals with shapes and solids. They all need an aptitude for concrete thinking.

Abstract thinking is the opposite of concrete thinking. When you are thinking abstractly, you are dealing with ideas rather than real objects. When a judge is weighing right against wrong, he is thinking abstractly. But when an architect is developing a house design, he is thinking concretely. Whether you are in the habit of thinking concretely or abstractly, it may prove helpful to consider both ways. There are teaching methods that aim to train the student along these lines. Some authorities believe that abstract thinking must follow concrete thinking.

Among the jobs that call for abstract thinking are those of lawyers, musicians, bankers, counselors, psychologists, ministers, priests, editorial writers, critics, and philosophy teachers. In fact, quite a number of vocations.

Both introverts and extroverts can rate high in either concrete thinking or abstract thinking. If you never made anything and can not take things apart and put them together again, you would probably rate low in concrete thinking. And if you usually settle arguments by deciding what is fair or unfair, this could indicate that you tend to think abstractly, in terms of ideas.

On the other hand, if you are the kind of person described as having finger skill (Chapter 7), with the ability to take things apart and put them together again, then you would probably score in concrete thinking.

How do you think you rate?

5 · Do You Enjoy Solving Puzzles?

Do you understand instructions easily? Can you quickly see what a collection of objects have in common? This common thing could be a spot of the same color, or a rounded corner, or maybe the same general shape. Are you a whiz at solving puzzles and riddles? Do you have intuition, that is, do you seem to "know" without having to think hard about something? In case your answer is "yes" to these questions, it is possible that you could score high in *inductive reasoning*—the ability to find the one explanation that fits a collection of assorted facts. This could be the general principle that accounts for these facts.

Newton used inductive reasoning to discover the principle of gravity. He first observed an apple falling. Then, watching other things fall, he was led to understand the force that caused objects to fall down instead of up. This force, known as gravity, is a general principle.

Persons who score high in inductive reasoning are urged to continue their schooling and develop a good vocabulary. Obviously, no one without inductive reasoning and a good vocabulary could expect to become a good lawyer. Most

Skill in inductive reasoning is one asset of the young manager shown at the right, greeting a visiting U.S. senator.

Johns-Manville Fibre Glass Division

successful lawyers and judges have high inductive reasoning, high abstract thinking, and an excellent vocabulary.

Who else needs this aptitude? Anyone in a job that calls for giving advice. A guidance counselor or a psychologist, for example, would need it. Others include the diagnostic physician, the college professor, the diplomat, the scientific researcher, the literary critic, the editorial writer, or the detective.

Jobs that investigate, research, gather facts, call for this aptitude. The people in an advertising agency who assemble all the facts about a product need this aptitude. They are seeking reasons to induce people to buy their product. When they find the one answer that fits the assorted facts about their product, they discover the best technique to advertise it.

Many jobs in scientific research call for this talent. A marine biologist who finds dead fish and discovers the polluting substance in the water that destroys marine life, is an example.

An extroverted person with this aptitude might make a good detective. This kind of person is able to organize activities that involve other people. For example, starting a union or a business, directing factory workers, managing a sales force, or supervising a crew on a building project.

The introverted person with good inductive reasoning would probably be happier doing the kind of research mentioned above, as well as laboratory testing, or compiling statistics in an insurance office. He would do well, also, as a materials tester in a factory, checking for quality and uniformity. It appears that persons with this aptitude, who also score high in concrete thinking, are the natural problem solvers. Tests seem to indicate that more women than men score high in inductive reasoning.

How would you rate yourself? The clues given may help you judge if you resemble any of the persons described.

6 · Are You Good at Organizing Your Thoughts?

Can you organize facts or your own thoughts and draw a logical conclusion from them? If you can, you would probably rate high in *deductive reasoning*—the ability to reach a conclusion from given facts. This is sometimes called *analytical reasoning,* the ability to analyze an idea or a principle in order to find its basic meaning.

Here is a simple example of deductive reasoning: "All dogs are animals. Lassie is a dog." From these facts you deduce that "Lassie is an animal."

The extroverted person with this aptitude is a good organizer and, in general, makes a good teacher. Assuming this person has the other necessary aptitudes, he or she could handle any job that calls for organizing thoughts, facts, or materials, quickly. A civil engineer, for example, must be able to survey the land and then design the basic parts of the highway he intends to build on that land. This means that he is able to organize the entire project by first seeing clearly, in his mind, how each part of the project is to be handled in building the highway.

The union leader or delegate has to use the same kind of

Deductive reasoning is useful in market research. *B. F. Goodrich*

reasoning. He must be able to see how the complaints or demands of the union members will fit in with the overall program he has organized. An accountant, too, must be able to organize the facts, or details, of a company's financial condition. This calls for deductive reasoning. Therefore, the introverted person, high in accounting aptitude and deductive reasoning, usually makes a fine accountant.

The detective, who examines clues in order to deduce what happened, is the classic example of someone who needs this aptitude.

A literary critic also needs deductive reasoning. He must

be able to analyze the book or article he is reviewing to see its components. The factory engineer, who has to plan a whole production line, uses deductive reasoning. A good automobile mechanic can listen to the sound of a motor and tell you what's wrong with it, thanks to his ability at deductive reasoning. These are a very few of the many jobs that call for people who can quickly see all the parts of a problem or project, arrange them in their minds, and find the right solution.

Some persons seem to be always mixed up, confused, unable to sort things out logically. Are you like this, or do you have a knack for organization? Can you arrange facts presented to you and draw a conclusion from them?

If the clues that have been given above seem to indicate that you do think this way, then perhaps you have an aptitude for deductive reasoning.

7 · Are You Handy or Awkward?

Are you "all thumbs" when you try to do things with your hands? Or are you a whiz at work or play that calls for using your fingers? Some persons are naturally handy with pliers, screwdrivers, crochet hooks, or knitting needles. Some are skillful at knotting string as in macramé, catching a ball, or making model airplanes. Others are always fumbling and dropping things. Which kind of person are you? If you are considered handy, you may have *finger skill*—the ability to manage or handle your fingers with ease and facility.

It is possible that more introverted than extroverted persons have good finger skill. Jobs that usually call for this aptitude include those in arts and crafts, cabinet making, and factory bench-assembly work with small, intricate parts. The concert pianist, the draftsman or layout artist, the printing pressman, the person in a laboratory working with a microscope, the occupational therapist, the jeweler, the photographer—all have jobs that call for good finger skill.

There are many different jobs for the extroverted person

Elmwood Elementary Schools

Interior designers who make models like this need finger skill.
Photo by Jack Senzer, Fashion Institute of Technology

who has this aptitude. Take, for instance, the factory foreman who trains others in bench-assembly work, or perhaps a salesroom demonstrator of sewing machines.

Since so many jobs call for finger skill, it is fortunate that many persons rate high in this aptitude. The introverted person is often quite happy doing work that calls for finger skill. The extroverted person, on the other hand, might become dissatisfied, and probably would prefer to work as a trainer or teacher of a particular skill. At some point this extroverted person would probably try to become a manager or supervisor, if he or she has the other aptitudes called for.

You should have little trouble deciding whether you have finger skill or not. If you carry a pocket knife regularly, and are able to take apart a toy or kitchen appliance and put it together again, the chances are you have finger skill. The same is true if you like to sew, crochet, or do stitchery, macramé, or other handicrafts.

If you think a particular job calls for this aptitude, first check your personality type. Will you be working by yourself? If you are introverted, well and good! However, if you consider yourself an extrovert, look for the kind of job that eventually could lead you into a training or supervisory position.

It is well to remember that very few jobs require only one aptitude. Virtually every job needs several aptitudes and skills. The last chapter will list all the aptitudes and typical jobs that call for them. The same job will be listed under several aptitudes, because it is a *combination* of aptitudes that must be considered.

8 · Are You Skillful With Small Tools?

Are your fingers really as nimble as you thought? Do you find it easy to grasp and work with a tiny needle? Does a pair of tweezers feel like an extension of your fingers, so that you find it easy to pick up tiny objects? Surprisingly, you could rate high in finger skill and still fumble over the delicate work that calls for *tweezer skill*—the ability to work with very small tools.

What job comes to mind first as suitable for such a skill? Isn't it dental work? A dentist has to have nimble fingers capable of grasping tiny instruments and tweezers which must become almost an extension of his fingers. But so must a draftsman, a jeweler, a factory bench-assembly worker on small parts, and a concert musician. The laboratory technician who uses a hypodermic needle and tiny slides to test blood samples, and the surgeon with a delicate touch, must have tweezer skill.

The work done by this technician in marine biology calls for tweezer dexterity. *Photo by V. Emerson Nulk. National Oceanic and Atmospheric Administration—U.S. Dept. of Commerce*

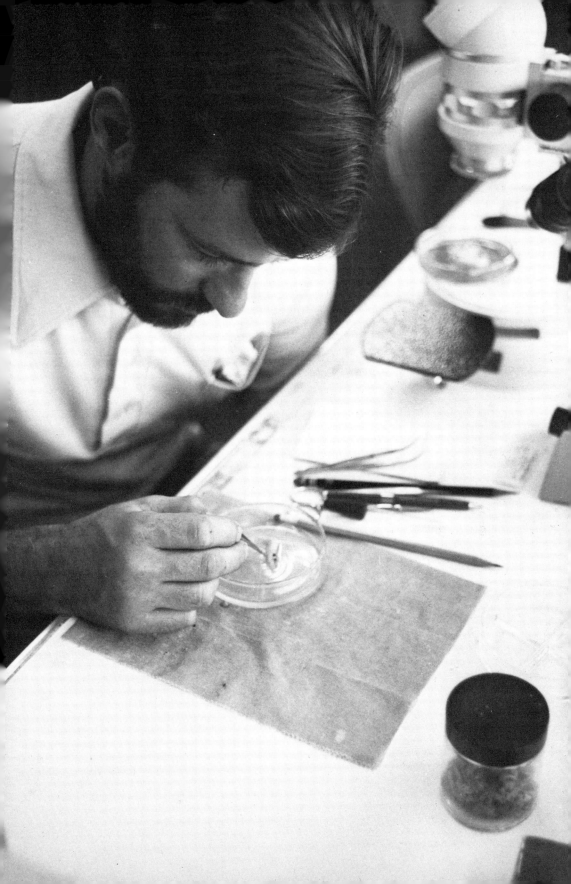

Every job that calls for working with your hands but using tweezers, tiny instruments, or fine tools, requires a high rating in this aptitude. Jobs of this kind are most often performed alone, or in a one-to-one situation as in a dentist's office. For this reason, they probably appeal more to the introverted person.

If you are extroverted and have this aptitude, you would do well to improve your vocabulary. Depending on your other aptitudes, this might help you toward a supervisory or managerial position. This aptitude would also be of great advantage to the extrovert who holds a job-training position—teaching others how to do the delicate work that requires tweezers or other fine instruments.

Today industry offers many jobs to people with a knack for handling fine tools. Toolmakers and diemakers are good examples. They make the tools that make the tiny parts for transistor radios, calculators, and similar products.

The operating-room nurse should have this ability, too. In hospital laboratories there are dozens of jobs that call for the skillful handling of tiny instruments. In manufacturing there are many production lines where bench-assembly workers must use small-scale tools to make even smaller products. Then there are product designers, and designers generally, who use tiny drawing instruments. Product engineers often make miniature models called prototypes. In construction there are architectural draftsmen, material testers, and chemical and other engineers who work with tiny test tubes, microscopes, and similar fine instruments.

Did you score yourself high in finger skill? Do you think,

now, that you also have tweezer skill? If you ever kept a stamp collection and used the small flat-nosed tweezers to move stamps around, you will be familiar with tweezers. Or, if you ever strung beads, made jewelry, handled wire sculpture, embroidered with fine needles, or made doll's clothes you would probably have this skill. If as a small child you learned to tie your shoelaces quickly and easily, this might be another clue.

Think about it. Decide whether you have that natural coordination in your fingers that is called tweezer skill.

9 · Do You Notice Details in the Things You See?

You might think that everyone ought to be able to look at something and remember what has been seen. But this is not so at all. When more than two people tell of something they have seen, their reports are often very different. Some people take in more of what they see than others. If you are quick to observe what is happening around you, and are able to remember many details, then you may have that aptitude called *observation*—the ability to take careful notice of details.

The first job this aptitude suggests is that of an inspector of quality control in a factory. Most manufacturing operations call for regular inspection in order to maintain quality of product. Almost everything that is manufactured or assembled is inspected before it is sent out to be sold. The person who makes this inspection must rate very high in observation ability. As with other aptitudes, this ability is sharpened by constant use and practice.

There are many jobs that call for good observation ability. These include the study of animals, insects, fish or other wildlife. Then there are those who study very tiny things like bacteria, using a microscope. There are jobs in

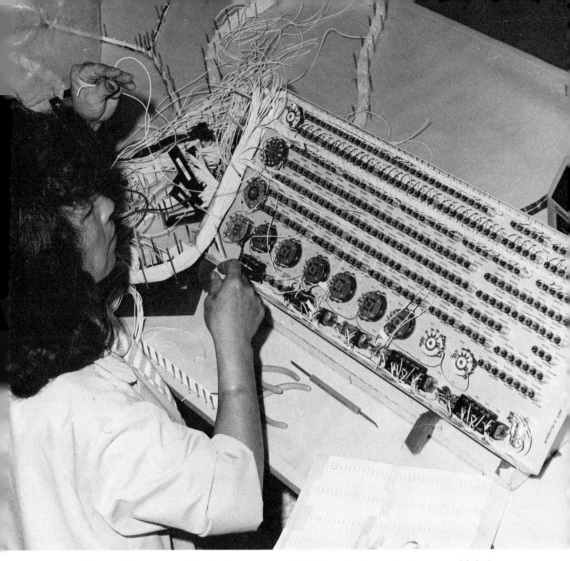

The quality control tester in a manufacturing plant needs to score high in observation. *National Cash Register Co.*

photography, writing, cartooning and illustration, designing, and newspaper reporting. And, of course, all jobs that call for research must focus on observation of many details.

The police should have good observation ability, and for the detective this aptitude is especially important. Detectives must be able to observe details that others overlook.

It is these clues that can help them solve a crime. Remember how Sherlock Holmes proved himself to be a first-rate observer?

It appears that this ability keeps developing in boys until the age of twenty. Then it remains the same for about ten years before it begins to decline. For some reason girls develop this ability sooner. They reach their top ability when they are about sixteen and remain at this level until they are about twenty-nine. Thereafter, this ability begins to decline as with men.

In case you are observant, you probably know it. But maybe you haven't thought much about it until now. Try to recall all the times you had to remember things that you saw. Were you good at recalling details? For example, if you rode on a bus to a ballgame, would you be able to remember the driver? Was he a black man or white? Did he have a beard or mustache or was he clean-shaven? Was the ticketseller tall or short? Was he wearing a coat, a sweater, or what? Did you see a policeman nearby? What did he look like? If you have observation ability, such details would tend to stay with you.

If you have this aptitude, try to develop it as much as possible. For example if you are interested in science, you might try to arrange to use a microscope. Think of the wonderful things you could do with it. A single drop of water, for instance, is full of fascinating objects. Such training could become valuable to you later. If a microscope is unavailable, perhaps you could visit the nearest natural history museum. Learn to observe well—and sharpen your learning with practice!

10 · Can You Remember Drawings, Cartoons, Pictures?

Can you close your eyes and "see" your favorite cartoons? Are you able to do the same with a diagram or the design on a rug, a blanket, or a poster? Can you look at a drawing and sketch it entirely from memory, even though you are not an artist? If you have this ability for observation, then you have a knack of remembering not only the details of what you saw, but the actual shape and form of every detail that makes up the design or picture. This talent is called *picture memory*—the ability to memorize drawings, designs, and pictures.

You might think that all artists have this ability, but that is not the case. The realistic landscape painter paints only what he sees before him. He may modify a little here and there to improve the design, perhaps, but he does not paint from memory. The portrait painter, too, paints only from the model who poses for him. Neither of these artists need picture memory because their art consists of their ability to copy that which is before them.

On the other hand, a cartoonist usually draws his pictures with no model in front of him. The only "copying" he does is to put on paper the image in his mind, something he remembers because of his picture memory. The knack of remembering shapes, designs, and pictures enables such a person to "see" images in his mind of people and objects, previously seen.

Memory for pictures is needed in many fields related to art. Aside from the professional cartoonist, there are many others who need this skill. Package designers, fashion designers, product designers of toys, appliances, electronic instruments and the like, all must have this special aptitude.

It is possible that most successful cartoonists and designers are more introverted than otherwise. Their work is usually solitary. However, some designers tend to be extroverts. They are often coordinators, commentators, or scouts, who travel and make sketches from memory of the designs and pictures they have seen at various shows and exhibits.

Other jobs calling for this aptitude would also involve some form of drawing or sketching. For instance, the architectural designer or draftsman has to create new forms or designs. The structural engineer has to make preliminary sketches of a new design. Exhibit designers, floral display designers, window display designers, stage or fashion designers, must create new designs, and they do this by calling on their memories for pictures stored there.

Like other aptitudes, this one is also sharpened with use and practice. It is one you should be able to recognize in

Good picture memory is helpful to designers and illustrators.
SUNY Fredonia, New York

yourself if you carefully think about it. Are you able to do any of the things described? If you score high in picture memory, the chances are you will rate high in concrete thinking. In that case, you would be well advised to go on with your education. Consider a career as an architectural designer or some other designing job discussed in this chapter.

Actually, it's best not to make a final decision about your choice of a cereer until you have full knowledge of all aptitudes. You will be able to plan better when you have completed the book and studied the listing of aptitudes in Chapter 21.

11 · Can You Remember Tunes?

Are you musically inclined? Can you carry a tune in your mind after you've heard it only once? Even though you may not play an instrument, can you hum along in tune with your favorite band? Do you often find yourself humming a tune that you have heard only briefly? If you can ·say "yes" to these questions, it may be that you have *tonal memory*—an ear for music because of your ability to remember sounds.

Persons with high scores in tonal memory frequently become interested in jobs or hobbies in the field of music or the performing arts. They have a natural gift for music and sometimes for composing, acting, and dancing. Such people find employment in radio or TV broadcasting, concert performing, recording, music teaching, as well as in photography or film making.

Individual performers tend to be introverted. Music salespeople, music teachers, directors, and the like, tend to be extroverted. In addition to tonal memory, usually a high creative imagination, high abstract thinking, and high accounting aptitudes are needed to become successful as a performer. Furthermore, for the topmost level of success, a superior vocabulary is absolutely necessary.

It is generally accepted that tonal memory is inherited. If your parents and grandparents were musical, then you stand a much better chance of also having this aptitude. But maybe you have resisted studying music or learning to play an instrument. Then the chances are that you are low in accounting aptitude and possibly in finger skill. To read notes fluently and to play an instrument well, you need both.

Now let's suppose you are an extrovert with a good tonal

A person with good tonal memory stands a better chance of becoming a good musician. *Sheldon Soffer Management*

memory and a high score in creative imagination and abstract thinking, but low in inductive reasoning. Well, then, you could be successful in selling music or musical instruments, or perhaps high-fidelity tape and record-sound equipment.

It should not be difficult for you to score yourself in this aptitude. Surely you know if you are musically inclined. Still, it is possible to have this aptitude, but because of your upbringing not to be fully aware of your musical talent. Stop to think about it carefully. Check the descriptions and clues, given above, and see if they apply to you.

If there is no doubt in your mind, you should look for that combination of aptitudes that point toward a career in music. The aptitudes that are important to a musician are as follows: tonal memory, finger skill, tweezer skill, abstract thinking, accounting aptitude, creative imagination, and possibly high-pitch awareness.

However, if you have tonal memory but very few of the other musical aptitudes, then it is best to consider your *dominant* aptitudes and follow their lead. Your tonal memory can be used in a hobby. You can enjoy it as an avocation rather than as a vocation.

12 · Do You Hear the Difference Between Sounds?

Now we come to a very specialized aptitude. Although it is important in the field of music, it is not limited to the musician. It has to do with a quality of the mind called *perception*. It is the ability to "know" or to "feel" and understand by means of your senses—a kind of sixth sense.

Suppose you are riding in an automobile and talking to your companion. You are not paying attention to the car, but suddenly you are aware that something is different. You stop talking to your companion for a moment, and then you know. The sound of the motor is different. No one hears it but you. You have that immediate or intuitive awareness that the motor is "off."

Is your ear so sharp that you can tell the difference between two sounds that are supposed to be identical? Or, in playing games where you don't think but guess, does your intuitive feeling often help you win? If the answer to these questions is "yes," it is possible you have *pitch awareness*. This is the ability to hear the difference between two notes of music that are meant to be identical.

A fine concert pianist has this highly refined quality of the senses. This special feeling for fine differences occurs in other areas besides music. For example, it may be found in exceptional photographers, distinguished actors, gifted doctors, brilliant research scientists. It is this outstanding talent that gives these persons a kind of sixth sense, which they use to great advantage in their work.

The successful acoustics engineer must have an especially keen ear. The medical internist who is considered exceptional applies this "sixth sense" to search out hidden diseases. The X-ray technician, if he is really good, uses this unique ability to interpret his photographic plates.

Some of the jobs that call for this aptitude are in broadcasting, music, dancing, acting, motion picture production and direction, playwriting, singing, and photography. This

The musical director usually has keen pitch awareness.

RCA Victor Records

aptitude can also be of benefit to judges. For them the ability to distinguish ideas and feelings is important.

There are jobs in industry that call for this special aptitude, too. And this feeling for fine differences is useful in surgery, psychological counseling, or research chemistry. It is an asset in all work that requires exceptionally creative or inventive minds.

It may be hard to know whether you have this special ability. Just stop and think. From the time you were a small child, were you interested in music and particularly sensitive to sounds? Was your hearing especially acute? Could you instantly tell how your mother felt, for example, by the sound of her voice? Well, then, perhaps you have this talent. If you do seem to have it, should you consider a career in music?

Your decision should depend on your combination of aptitudes. Find out what your *dominant* aptitudes are. If they are not in music, but you do have pitch awareness, this talent, plus other aptitudes, will give you special ability in any career for which you are fitted.

13 · Can You Keep Time With Music?

When you hear a band playing, do you automatically tap your feet or fingers in time with the rhythm? Is it easy for you to learn dance steps? When walking alongside someone, do you unconsciously alter your stride to keep in step? If these things come to you naturally, it is possible that you have *rhythm memory*—the ability to keep time with music.

This aptitude is absolutely necessary for anyone who expects to play drums, or be in the rhythm section of a band. It is also useful to anyone in a job that calls for rhythmic movements. A dancer, amateur or professional, must have this ability in order to perform well. However, there are also factory jobs that require rhythmic movement. The worker who is feeding a production line needs it. A bagel or pretzel maker twirls his dough in rhythm with a moving belt. Workers on fast production lines must develop their rhythmic movements to keep pace with the moving belt.

Virtually every job in the music field calls for this aptitude. In fact, jobs that call for rhythm spread into all fields, from the performing arts to construction and manufacturing. Ice skaters, circus performers, baton twirlers, have this

Pop groups often feature drums and the player who rates high in rhythm memory.   *Plainview-Old Bethpage, New York Public Schools*

ability in common with machine operators, typists, and all those who have to move their bodies or their hands and fingers to keep pace with certain movements. Both introverted and extroverted persons may have this aptitude.

If you are musically inclined, and hope to make music your career, you would certainly need this aptitude. But a great many persons who have a good sense of rhythm do not become professional performers. Among them are the music lovers who make up the audiences. They come to watch and listen to professional performers, and their en-joyment is greatly increased because of their feeling for rhythm.

If you have good rhythm, you have a gift that can add zest to your life. You will always be able to enjoy music, to dance with greater pleasure, and perhaps to sing or play an instrument. What's more, if your job calls for keeping time with certain movements, you will be able to perform more skillfully. For example, this ability may improve your tennis or golf game, or make you a better swimmer.

How do you know if you have rhythm memory? Study all the clues given above. And if you don't have two "left feet" when learning to dance, and if you automatically keep time with the rhythmic sound of a band, then you probably have your share of rhythm memory.

14 · Can You Tell the Difference Between Two Musical Notes?

Here's a simple test you might take. Listen to two trumpet players, both playing the same tune. Can you tell if one of the trumpets has a different tone quality from the other? Tone quality is the natural vibration of the sound. We call it "resonance," the way the tone affects our ears. If your hearing is sharp enough to tell such differences, you may have *timbre awareness*—the ability to tell the difference between two musical notes with the same pitch and volume.

Great conductors have this talent. When the famous Toscanini rehearsed his orchestra, he would abruptly stop when his sensitive ear picked up a single note that lacked proper timbre or resonance. He would point an accusing finger at the luckless musician who would feel demolished.

But this aptitude has meaning beyond music. It is also the special talent of the engineer, for instance, who can listen to the sound of a machine and suddenly sense that something is wrong. His "fine" ear has detected a sound that is not resonant, but of a different timbre.

Walter Suskind is typical of the director with good timbre awareness.
Photo by T. Mike Fletcher, St. Louis Symphony Orchestra

This special ability is found in certain gifted persons in jobs where they must judge sounds. The acoustical engineer should have this aptitude. So, too, should the high-fidelity salesman and the electronic expert who must pass judgment on the sounds produced. Music critics must be able to evaluate musical performances. Operatic singers must not only hear the timbre of every note, but must be able to produce it perfectly. Anyone who deals with tonal quality and who is connected in some professional way with the musical field, needs this aptitude.

As with pitch awareness, this talent indicates a "special feeling" for fine differences. It amounts to a sharpened perception or a "sixth sense." Persons especially gifted in their individual fields—great surgeons, for example—have this special feeling that makes them superior to the average surgeon. The research scientist who has this talent might make great discoveries. And an automobile mechanic with timbre awareness could "sense" immediately the problem with a car motor.

Let's assume you have this awareness without other musical abilities. In that case, you should consider the dominant aptitudes in your particular combination. This special ability could enhance your other aptitudes and thus heighten the quality of your work.

Unless you are musical and are already playing an instrument, you may not be able to judge if you really have this aptitude. However, if you are musical, and you believe you do have this talent, it would be wise to continue study in whatever musical field appeals to you. In any event, it will pay to develop your vocabulary. A sound knowledge of language is always a plus!

15 · Can You Remember Telephone Numbers?

Scientists who study the brain have discovered the way we remember things. We have, according to them, a short-term memory and a long-term memory. The short-term memory is used when we remember a telephone number just long enough to dial it. However, if that number is important, and we have need to call it often, it slips into another area of the mind which is called "long-term memory." Some of us are better than others in both these memory areas. What about you? If you can recall telephone numbers, dates, addresses, and the like, this points to the special aptitude of remembering a great many facts and details.

Is it easy for you to remember the dates of your relatives' or friends' birthdays? Can you recall, instantly, the prices of grocery items? What about numbers on automobile license plates? Where did you place that book on birds? And on what street did you see a maple tree in brilliant autumn color? Can you remember all the details and describe the style of the dress you saw in the display window —the kind of collar, the cut of the skirt, whether belted or not? How many details of the street accident you witnessed

The computer programmer needs good number memory.

can you remember later? If you can recall details such as these, then you probably have *number memory*—the ability to remember numbers and retain a great many details.

This very useful aptitude is found in both introverted and extroverted persons. Typical jobs that call for this talent are those of the museum curator, and the librarian, who have to keep a vast number of details and facts in mind. Then there is the factory production manager who must juggle schedules and constantly balance them against orders and deliveries. The bookstore manager, too, must not only remember what a book is about, on any subject, but where it may be found and the number on its cover.

Then there's the stock-market operator. He must combine his number memory with all the details of the up-or-down movement of hundreds of stocks. And the stockroom clerk must have ready answers to questions about a great many items in his stockroom. A variety of jobs, of which these are a few, call for this talent to remember numbers and many details.

From all these clues and descriptions, you may be able to judge whether you have number memory. If you think you have, and you are an introvert, you should consider this in relation to your other aptitudes. Try to understand how this can further your career. For example, if you also score high in concrete thinking and finger skill, you might choose a job in research, or one in drafting in the construction field.

The extrovert, on the other hand, would do well to take a job working with others, possibly in a managerial, teaching, or administrative area. The possibilities abound. But remember, it is the *combination* of your aptitudes that will determine the direction you should follow in choosing your career.

16 · Have You a Good Eye for Pleasing Arrangements?

Anyone who works in the field of commercial art should have a "good eye." Do you have this gift? Can you look at drawings, made up of different shapes and arranged in groups, and pick out the one arrangement likely to appeal to most people? Maybe you are the kind of person who prefers to change the groups around, so as to get a better arrangement. If you have the knack of picking out the design or layout of a group of objects in a picture or in a room that generally pleases people, then perhaps you have *popular proportion aptitude*. This is the ability to see and recognize eye-appealing and harmonious proportions of a given object.

Outstanding architects do not use this aptitude. They aren't interested in arrangements or designs that are pleasing to most people. Rather, they want to create designs that are new and challenging. Witness the Guggenheim Museum on Fifth Avenue in New York City. This striking design is the work of the great architect, Frank Lloyd Wright.

A floral designer needs the knack of making arrangements that are likely to please most people.   *Beatrice Criner*

When this building was erected, its design was considered very strange to most people. But it is hailed today as a magnificent architectural achievement.

On the other hand, commercial artists, package designers, layout artists, stage designers, fashion designers, to mention only a few, all need popular proportion aptitude. To be successful in their various fields, they must be able to please the majority of the public.

Fine artists, unlike those in the commercial field, might score high in picture memory, observation and finger skill, and not have the popular proportion aptitude at all. Usually they are introverted, and tend to be individualistic. They are happy only when they are expressing *themselves*, whether it is likely to please others or not.

How would you rate yourself in popular proportion aptitude? Do you have a feeling for nice things? Do you like to rearrange furniture in a room for a more pleasing effect? Perhaps you are talented in art and have already made posters or decorations that people like and admire. In that case, you probably have this aptitude.

The introverted person fits more readily into this group of artists and designers. If you are an extrovert who scores high in this aptitude, you would probably do best in such a field as civil engineering. There you would be in contact with many people while you design highways and bridges or public buildings. Again, you might do well as an interior designer in the furniture field, perhaps selling to people who would look to you for guidance. You could use this talent in photography or as a film director. Here, too, it would be wise to develop a large vocabulary. Top jobs in these fields call for the ability to express oneself well.

17 · Are You Interested in Words and Language?

Do you like to read? Are you fond of crossword puzzles and games like Scrabble? Can you remember unfamiliar words? Were you a good student in English? If you ever studied another language, did you find it interesting and, fairly easy? If you can say "yes" to these questions, it is likely that you have the aptitude for *language learning*. This is the ability to learn a language, or to remember technical words and phrases.

The importance of a good vocabulary has been mentioned several times. Experience has shown that to get to the top in any field, a large vocabulary is vital. This is especially important if you score high in deductive reasoning. It is impossible to make full use of your deductive abilities without the background of knowledge that is acquired as you develop an ever-increasing vocabulary. In industry, as in the professions, every important executive, administrative, or managerial job requires this aptitude.

Fortunately, it's an ability that can be developed. There are many ways of improving your vocabulary. One good way is to read good books with a dictionary at your side.

Look up every word that is unfamiliar to you, that you do not now use. Study the way it is used, both in the book and in the dictionary. Then repeat the word, aloud, in a sentence you would use when talking to someone. In this way you will become familiar with the sound, as well as the definition. Include it in your conversation at the first opportunity. It will soon become part of your oral vocabulary. The more words you add to your list, the better you will be able to think, and the better you will become in communicating your ideas to others.

Aptitudes are special talents with which we are born. Under the right conditions and with practice, they develop

People in executive jobs usually have good language learning skills.
Farm and Power Equipment Magazine

and become special skills. Knowledge is something we must acquire. This comes as we work and study to gain a large vocabulary. Therefore, an aptitude for language learning is a great asset. Studies made of persons who were tested for their aptitudes have shown that a good vocabulary is vital to gaining success in any field. Success is not only financial reward but, more important, the satisfaction that comes with personal fulfillment.

There are many success stories of people with little education who nevertheless managed to achieve success and even fame. A study of their lives shows that they lacked only formal schooling. Actually, they educated themselves. Thomas Edison is a good example. He had little formal schooling and was taught by his mother. Yet, at the time of his death in 1931, he was acclaimed by the whole world as one of its most brilliant men. He had developed over 1,300 patents. His education was based on everyday experience. But over the years he developed a vocabulary that helped him in his outstanding career.

How do you rate yourself in learning words and language? Do you shy away from books and reading? Or are you interested in gaining knowledge by reading books? A good vocabulary is equally needed by introverted and extroverted persons.

18 · Do You Think About the Future?

Do you think about what lies ahead of you? Do you plan for it? Would you go off on a camping trip without first planning for every possible happening? Or would you think about each day's activity and list everything you might need: a flashlight, an axe, a tent, cooking utensils, rope, and so on. If you naturally think things out first, planning for whatever may happen tomorrow and the days after, you may have the aptitude called *foresight*. This is the ability to give careful thought to the future.

Being a worrier is not the same as having foresight. This simply means that you have a "hangup." The person with foresight usually is deliberate rather than impulsive. Such a person generally has good judgment and persistence, a kind of stick-to-itiveness. He or she has the habit of thinking about the past, present and future as they relate to each other. A person like this can set up reasonable goals.

Those low in foresight may give up on things more or less on impulse. In school they may start one course and then, impulsively, drop out of it. Small, immediate obstacles appear to be impossibly difficult.

The best lawyers, who are usually introverted, have good foresight. They need it because their work demands many hours of patient study and research. Also they have to give advice which often affects their client's future. Good executives, and others in administrative or managerial positions, need foresight as well. The jobs of many people under their direction often depend on their judgment and ability to look ahead.

Many kinds of jobs call for this aptitude; for instance, those that involve production and factory planning. Here

All planning jobs call for the use of foresight.

the ability to foresee public demand is required. The sudden energy crisis that struck the world in 1973-1974 is a prime example of the lack of foresight by many persons in the highest places. Had government leaders and oil industry executives used more foresight, the crisis might have been avoided.

This is an aptitude found in introvert and extrovert alike. What about you? Would you score yourself high or low in foresight? Think back over your life. When it was necessary for you to plan for something that could happen in the future, did you do so? If you are fair in judging yourself, you should be able to tell by past experience whether or not you have this highly desirable quality.

19 · Can You Tell Red from Green?

This is one aptitude that can be quickly determined. Many persons have this aptitude only partially, and some lack it completely. Can you tell the difference between red and green, between blue and yellow? When you drive a car and come to a stop light, do you see the colors as they are— green or red—or do you see them in shades of gray? If you can clearly see all colors from red to violet, there is no doubt that you have good *color perception*—the ability to distinguish all colors correctly.

Those without this ability are classified as color-blind. This inherited visual defect of the male sex can be partial or total. When it is total, no colors can be seen. Vision is limited to seeing everything in shades of gray. It's like the difference between a color photograph and a black-and-white picture of the same subject, or the difference between color TV and black-and-white TV. A red color in the scene would appear as a deeper shade of gray. The blues would appear light by comparison. All other colors would fall in between, in varying shades of gray.

It is possible to be partially color-blind without knowing

it. The reason for this is that the human mind can make amazing adjustments. Over the years, one may learn how to "see" colors, not by normal color perception but by interpreting tonal values. However, partial color-blindness can be detected. So, too, can the most common form of partial color-blindness known as red-green blindness. This is the inability to see the difference between red and green. The rarer form of color-blindness is called blue-yellow color-blindness, an inability to see the difference between the colors blue and yellow. Where there is a relatively unimportant question of color, such as the difference between black ink and red, the color-blind person would notice the difference in shades of black and gray. In any case, this lack may appear in both introverted or extroverted persons but, as previously noted, only in the male sex.

Obviously, jobs that require color recognition would be barred to those who have this affliction. Jobs in dress designing, color coordinating, interior design and decoration; even factory bench-assembly work, where tiny parts and wires are color-coded, would be outside their ability.

Luckily, there are plenty of other jobs that do not call for color perception. Examples are the jobs of accountants, bookkeepers, clerks, secretaries, office managers, telephone operators, and manufacturing or construction work where color is not a factor.

If you lack color perception in part, or in whole, then you must accept this fact and learn to avoid situations where colors are important.

A dress designer needs good color perception.

SUNY Fredonia, New York

20 · How Do You Think You Score?

To repeat, no book on aptitudes can take the place of actual testing. Taking a series of aptitude tests can be one of the most important steps you will ever take in planning for your future. However, reading about aptitudes will give you at least some idea of your own tendencies and natural abilities.

In case testing is not available to you, review very carefully the list of aptitudes that follows. Then score yourself as fairly and honestly as possible.

Write at the top of a sheet of paper the kind of personality you think you have, mostly introvert or mostly extrovert. Then jot down the numbers 1 to 19 in a column on the left side of the paper. Next, write beside each number what you think your score is for that particular aptitude—high, medium, or low.

Ask someone else to score you, too, preferably someone who knows you well. This might be a relative, a friend, a teacher, your minister, or your school guidance counselor. Finally, compare the results and discuss them with this other person.

Your Aptitudes

1. *Personality Pattern:* Mostly introvert; mostly extrovert.
2. *Accounting Aptitude:* The ability to handle all kinds of paper work.
3. *Creative Imagination:* The ability to develop lots of ideas.
4. a. *Concrete Thinking:* The ability to think or imagine solid objects.
   b. *Abstract Thinking:* The ability to think along non-material lines.
5. *Inductive Reasoning:* The ability to find a logical answer when you are faced with only scattered facts.
6. *Deductive Reasoning:* The ability to organize material, so that a principle can be reduced to its basic parts.
7. *Finger Skill:* The ability to use your fingers with skill.
8. *Tweezer Skill:* The ability to work with very small tools.
9. *Observation:* The ability to note details in what you see.
10. *Picture Memory:* The ability to memorize designs, pictures.
11. *Tonal Memory:* The ability to remember sounds; an ear for music.
12. *Pitch Awareness:* The ability to tell the difference between two notes of music meant to be identical.
13. *Rhythm Memory:* The ability to keep time with music.
14. *Timbre Awareness:* The ability to tell the difference between two musical notes with the same pitch and volume.

15. *Number Memory:* The ability to remember numbers and keep a great many details in mind.
16. *Popular Proportion Aptitude:* The ability to see pleasing and harmonious proportions.
17. *Language Learning:* The ability to learn a new language or to remember technical words; vocabulary-building.
18. *Foresight:* The ability to give careful thought to what is ahead.
19. *Color Perception:* The ability to see differences between all colors.

21 Aptitudes and Typical Jobs that Call for Them

Once you are tested, either in a testing laboratory or by a vocational guidance counselor, you will be counseled afterward. First, you will be asked what kind of job you think suits you best. One young man, who had taken this test, said he thought he would like to be an accountant. His test scores were as follows:

Creative Imagination	High
Abstract Thinking	High
Finger Skill	High
Language Learning	High
Concrete Thinking	Low
Accounting Aptitude	Low
Personality Pattern	Introvert

His test administrator pointed out that he lacked the primary qualification of a good accountant. He was low in accounting aptitude. Then, each of his aptitudes was discussed, according to the typical job list given below. It soon became clear that he would do well in some field of writing. The young man then recalled that he had had great interest in English and had earned high marks in composition. The recommendation that he explore the writing field appealed to him.

Study the following listing of jobs under each aptitude. Remember it is your combination of aptitudes you must consider, as the young man did above. Review the kind of jobs under each aptitude. Then find those which call for your dominant aptitudes.

For example, suppose you score yourself high in accounting aptitude, concrete thinking, inductive reasoning, but low or medium in all others. Look for those jobs listed under each of your dominant aptitudes. Chances are you may discover one or more jobs that appeal to you. Remember, it isn't possible to list every job in every category. The jobs shown are typical, and these should suggest similar ones that may not be listed.

Let us say that you like drafting. Think about your aptitudes. Do you lean toward the scientific, perhaps construction work, rather than toward business or manufacturing? If you did well in your studies of science and mathematics, then you may be on the right track. Turn to the descriptions of your dominant aptitudes. Checking accounting aptitude, we find that drafting is listed. Under concrete thinking, drafting is also listed. However, it is not shown under inductive reasoning. But you learned in Chapter 5 that this aptitude is useful for jobs in scientific research, investigating, gathering facts. Before a draftsman can begin to design, he has to gather all the facts. He then proceeds to create the design which will accommodate these facts. It would therefore appear that drafting would be a good job choice to investigate.

In any event, this should only be tentative. Do not make any final conclusions at this point. You should find out as much as you possibly can about any job you think would suit you.

Aptitudes and Typical Jobs That Call for Them

Accounting Aptitude: accounting, actuarial work (usually insurance statistics), auditing, banking, working as a bank teller, bookkeeper, business-machine operator, handling clerical duties, including filing. Also concert piano playing, music conducting, economics reporting, drafting, engineering (electrical, mechanical, civil); financial reporting, insurance accounting, international finance counseling, general investment research and counseling, nursing, most office jobs including stenography and secretarial work, organ and piano playing, record keeping, working as a statistician, working as a comptroller or treasurer in a corporation or trust company, or the like. In a word, jobs that call for the ability to handle all kinds of figures and paper work.

Creative Imagination: advertising, working as an artist, composing music, interviewing, radio and TV announcing, creating sales and promotional campaigns, business advising, cartooning, teaching, consulting, working in architecture, professional dancing, designing, editorial and copy writing, selling, merchandising, handling public relations, working as an occupational therapist, theatrical work from stage design to directing, all kinds of writing, including fiction and nonfiction, and so on. In summary, jobs that call for the ability to create lots of ideas.

Concrete Thinking: acoustical engineering, aeronautical engineering and designing, aircraft maintenance, all fields of engineering, working as an archaeologist, architectural designing, working as an astronomer, an anatomist, a researcher in biology or chemistry, clay modeling, commercial and interior designing, composing music, die-making, drafting, scientific experimenting, assembling products in a factory, geological researching, working in horticulture or in a laboratory, researching in the medical field, working in meteorology, in microscopy, sculpturing, surgery, dentistry. In short, jobs calling for the ability to imagine real objects, whether solid or three-dimensional.

Abstract Thinking: accounting, acting, advising/counseling, advertising, banking, bookkeeping, working as a clerk, teaching, radio and TV announcing and commentating, composing music, concert piano playing, creative or editorial writing, literary and dramatic criticism, professional dancing, working as an executive, financial and governmental work, diplomacy, group influencing, as in politics and public relations, historical research, all professions which may be classified as intellectual, such as psychotherapy, law, mathematics, all facets of music, selling, secretarial and statistical work, teaching, etc. All these jobs require the ability to think in terms of ideas rather than objects.

Inductive Reasoning: advertising, advising/counseling, archaeology, biological or chemical research, teaching, news commentating or reporting, critical or editorial writing, diagnostic medicine, psychotherapy, diplomacy, theatre direction, dramatic criticism, experimental science, geological surveying, policy-making positions in government, group influencing, historical research, international law and the study of jurisprudence, mathematics, medical research, musical criticism, physiological research, planning the sales and promotion of any product, playwriting, journalism, product supervising, statistical research, etc. Such jobs demand an ability to find a logical reason or general principle to account for a collection of assorted facts.

Deductive Reasoning: accounting, advertising, biological research, composing music, newspaper work, critical or editorial writing, journalism, mathematics, medical research, musical criticism, physiological research, planning jobs of all kinds, teaching, most kinds of writings, etc. All these jobs call for the ability to organize material, so that a complicated idea or a principle can be reduced to its basic parts.

Finger Skill: all kinds of arts and crafts, assembly work or bench work in a factory, modeling, sculpting, perform-

ing on any musical instrument, making jewelry, laboratory work in general, medical research, microscopy, occupational therapy, photography, handling materials
and recognizing textures, virtually all trades. Such jobs
require the ability to manage or handle your fingers with
ease and facility.

Tweezer Skill: architectural design, bacteriology, biological research, concert performing on most musical instruments, creative art, drafting and graphic design, experimental science, the work of a laboratory technician,
medical research, nursing, dentistry, physiological research, surgery, factory bench-assembly work. In fact,
any trade or job that requires delicacy of touch and the
ability to work with very small tools.

Observation: studying animal, insect, or fish life as a natu-
ralist, all forms of art expression, bacteriological and
other scientific research, microscopy, dramatics, editorial and critical writing, factory-production inspection,
journalism and newspaper reporting, medical and similar kinds of research, the work of a museum curator,
motion picture direction, still and motion picture photography, fiction and nonfiction writing, etc. These jobs
demand an ability to take careful notice of all details
under your observation.

Picture Memory: architectural designing, all aspects of designing including commercial, package, stage, dress, and
engineering design; cartooning, etc. These jobs make use
of the ability to memorize drawings, designs, pictures.

Tonal Memory: needed in all phases of music, composing,

playing, singing, all theatrical activities, dancing, and acting as well. Also needed in acoustical engineering, radio, and TV broadcasting engineering, all areas of sound production such as high fidelity manufacturing and selling, and in photography. Such jobs require an ear for music and the ability to remember sounds.

Pitch Awareness: musical accompanying, acoustical engineering, acting, broadcasting, both radio and TV, composing music, concert performing, dancing and dramatics, playing any instrument, musical criticism, high fidelity manufacturing and selling, recording on tapes and records, etc. All these jobs call for the ability to hear the difference between two notes of music that are meant to be identical. This aptitude is also found in the gifted scientist, the exceptional surgeon, the distinguished actor. They all share a sixth sense in the creative area.

Rhythm Memory: composing music, concert piano playing, professional dancing, musical criticism, and especially playing an instrument in the rhythm section of a band or orchestra. Rhythm memory is useful to the listener as well as to the performer. The ability to keep time with music is important in these jobs.

Timbre Awareness: differs from pitch awareness in that the ear is capable of detecting a very subtle difference in the vibration of certain musical notes or sounds with the same pitch and volume. It belongs in the same grouping of jobs listed for pitch awareness. However, the person who has this special talent has a very keen sense of perception and an unusual gift for observing "fine" differences. This makes him eligible for jobs that call for the ability to tell the difference between two musical notes with the same pitch and volume.

Number Memory: work of a museum curator, a librarian, one who expedites factory production, works at jobs in the field of investment, insurance, or the stock market, where numbers are all important. Telephone operators, train dispatchers, meteorologists, production schedulers in factories would qualify. They must have the ability to remember numbers and keep a great many details in mind.

Popular Proportion Aptitude: advertising and other forms of commercial art, designing in all areas including interiors, stage, packaging, fashion, architecture, photography, etc. Applicants for these jobs should have the ability to see and recognize pleasing and harmonious proportions that appeal to most people.

Language Learning: needed in all top-level jobs, such as those held by an executive, a manager or administrator. Also the person who has the job of influencing groups, such as a sales-training expert, a public relations director, a teacher, and a lecturer. Professional persons in psychology, medicine, engineering, chemistry, law, and ministry also qualify. What is needed is the ability to learn a new language, or to remember technical words and phrases.

Foresight: Lawyers, executives, persons in administrative positions, diplomats, product and production planners, meteorologists, and all persons in jobs that forecast needs and trends. In short, those who have to think and plan ahead to meet the problems they foresee. They are likely to do well in jobs that call for an ability to give careful thought to whatever may be ahead in the future.

Color Perception: artists, clothing designers, stage designers, photographers, everyone who must be able to see and work with colors. In such jobs, one must be able to see the differences between all colors.

22 · Preparing a Resumé and Applying for a Job

Before you begin to apply for any job, you should get all the information you can about the industry itself. And you should find out what you can about some of the companies and organizations within this industry.

After you collect the names of companies in the industry, write to the Public Relations Department of each company. Ask for their literature, the printed matter that describes the company and its work. Study this literature carefully.

You may decide that this industry doesn't appeal to you, after all, or the information may spur you on and stimulate your imagination.

If you feel you have the right combination of aptitudes for a particular job and you want to apply for it, it is a good idea to prepare a resumé of your background.

The resumé should summarize your past experiences and your qualifications for the job. In case this is the first real job you have ever applied for, the following format would be suitable.

Resumé

John J. Doe
Street Address
City and State
Telephone Number

Age: _____
Height: _____
Weight: _____
Health: _____

Education: List the school or schools attended, the subjects in which you majored. Point out those that relate to the job for which you are applying and your grades (if they were good).

Extracurricular Activities: List the clubs, groups, activities, in which you participated. Give all pertinent details; for example, if you were the editor of the school paper, president of the student council, leader in the debating club, etc. Give this a lot of thought because such activities, even if limited only to sports, can give a more interesting picture of you as an individual.

Job Experience: List here, in chronological order, whatever jobs you held during summer vacations. These could be working as a camp counselor, supermarket clerk, newspaper delivery, golf caddy, babysitter, etc. Try to tell how each job helped you to mature, become more responsible; how these jobs helped develop you as a person.

Aptitudes: If you were tested professionally, tell where. This will give you the best chance to explain how your aptitudes fit you for the job. If you were not tested professionally, state what you believe your strengths are, based on what you have learned from this book.

Recommendations and References: Give the names, titles, and addresses of three responsible persons with whom you have had contact, and who are able to give you a character reference. These can be your former employers, or a teacher, school counselor, minister, or any prominent person who knows you. Do not list any relatives.

This resumé is to be sent with a letter of application, such as the suggested form given below.

A Sample of Application to Accompany Resumé

Date _____

Name of Employer (or Personnel Manager)
Name of Company
Address

Dear Mr. _____

    I am applying for the position of ____*(give job title here)*____ My qualifications and references are listed in the accompanying resumé.

    I have been preparing myself for a career in this field, as you will note from the listing of my study majors. Please note, also, that my aptitudes indicate that I should be able to perform the duties of this job to your satisfaction.

    May I have the opportunity to discuss this application with you in a personal interview?

    Thank you for your consideration.

                    Sincerely yours,
                    (your signature)

Alternate Form if You Were
Not Tested Professionally

Dear Mr. _____

    I am applying for the position of _____*(give job title here)*_____
My qualifications and references are listed in the accompanying resumé.

    I have been preparing myself for a career in this field, following a study of my aptitudes. In my judgment, and with the help of objective counsel, I believe I have the qualifications required to perform to your satisfaction the duties of this particular job.

    May I have the opportunity to discuss this application with you in a personal interview?

    Thank you.

Sincerely yours,

NOTE: Both the resumé and letter should be typed, if possible. If you cannot do this yourself, find someone who can do it for you. If you are not in a city where typing services are available, request help from a minister, a teacher, a counselor. Perhaps your brother or sister or your parents may know someone who is a typist. You will find that people will be willing to help, particularly for such a good cause.

    Services in the larger cities prepare such resumés and provide sufficient copies to mail to a number of companies. It is probably a good idea to select several companies in the same field. If you send only one letter, it is possible that the company you chose may not have such a position available, and your letter may go unanswered.

Suggested Resumé for Veterans
of the Armed Forces

RESUME

John J. Doe   Age: _____
Street Address   Height: _____
City and State   Weight: _____
Telephone Number   Health: _____

Education: List the school or schools attended, the subjects in which you majored (especially if they relate to the job for which you are applying), and your grades.

Extracurricular Activities: List the clubs, groups, activities, in which you were interested while at school. Give any pertinent details, such as being the editor of the school paper, president of the student counsel, leader in the debating club, etc. Give this a lot of thought because such activities, even if limited to sports, can give a more interesting picture of you as an individual.

Job Experience: List whatever jobs you held, chronologically, giving a brief description of the duties of each, the name of the company and address, and the name of your superior.

Armed Forces and Special Skills Gained: Give all the details of your service in the armed forces: branch, rank, duties, especially if you were part of a service group, or were assigned to some particular job for which training was received. Try to relate this experience and training to the job for which you are applying.

Aptitudes: See both previous resumés and use the one

which fits your case. Be sure to stress how these aptitudes best fit you for the job.

References: List the names of all previous employers, and names, titles, and addresses of three persons who are able to give you a character reference.

NOTE: A returned veteran frequently presents himself to the Personnel Manager without the formality of a mailed application, asking for an interview. In such a case, you should have this resumé with you, folded neatly in an envelope. Present this to the person who interviews you at the start of the interview itself. If a letter is required, either one of the two forms given previously may be used.

Index